# THE GOLDEN YEARS

# 1953

**text:** David Sandison

**design:** Paul Kurzeja

SIENA

D1420969

**195**

A tumultuous year by any standards, 1953 was marked by any number of arrivals and departures which would prove historically important, and a handful of achievements which would also leave indelible prints in the sands of time.

Least unmourned departure of the year - if not the century - was the death of Soviet dictator Josef Stalin, a monster whose crimes against the people of the USSR placed him alongside Adolf Hitler in the world's pantheon of shame. His passing signalled the arrival of Nikita Khrushchev, a new broom who'd prove as capable of sending up a cloud of blinding Cold War dust as he was of sweeping away the debris left by Stalin.

Arrivals included President Eisenhower, whose distinguished military past guaranteed the United States an administration determined to reinforce the nation's status as leader of the free world; Queen Elizabeth II, whose youth and enthusiasm would give Britain a model figurehead as it tried to shake off its patriarchal and parochial past to establish its world role in the second half of the century. Meanwhile, in Washington, the Supreme

Court began to unravel the complexities of 19th century race laws which had created second-class citizenship - or worse - for generations of black people. Raising alarm in conservative southern whites, it raised hope in the hearts of those working for true equality.

Medical science provided the two breakthroughs which would transform our lives. Jonas Salk's polio vaccine would eliminate a killer, while success in identifying and describing DNA - the basic building block of life - would give other scientists and doctors the opportunity to find cures to many more diseases. All in all, it was a very good year.

## Double RAF Celebrations

The Royal Air Force had two reasons to extend New Year celebrations early this month.

On January 1, Arthur 'Bomber' Harris, wartime head of the RAF's Bomber Command, a vital arm in the Allies' eventual victory over Hitler, was awarded a knighthood in the Queen's first New Year Honours List.

A day later, personnel at the RAF airbase at Abingdon, Oxfordshire, took delivery of their first supersonic aircraft - 400 US-designed Sabre jet fighters.

# Paris Waits For Godot

Parisian theatre-goers had a fresh experience this evening when *Waiting For Godot,* the newest and most challenging play from the pen of Irish-born Samuel Beckett, was given its world premiere. Reviews of the surreal dialogue between two tramps (Godot never arrives) were mixed, some hailing it as a 'Theatre of the Absurd' masterpiece and others dismissing it as rubbish.

# No Reprieve: Bentley Hanged For Cop Killing

DESPITE A LAST-MINUTE CALL from 200 Members of Parliament that he be reprieved, 19 year old Derek Bentley was hanged at London's Wandsworth Prison today for complicity in the fatal shooting of police constable Sidney Miles by 16 year old Christopher Craig.

During the men's trial in December 1952, Lord Chief Justice Goddard described Craig as 'one of the most dangerous criminals ever to stand in the dock' of the Central Criminal Court. Because of his age, Craig avoided the death penalty and was sentenced to be detained at Her Majesty's pleasure.

Despite evidence that Bentley was in the safe custody of police at the moment Craig fired nine shots at PC Miles with his .45 revolver, and dispute whether his shout of 'Let him have it Chris!' was a request for Craig to hand his gun over or - as the prosecution claimed – an order for Craig to shoot, Bentley was found guilty of murder.

His death sentence came despite a jury recommendation for mercy. It was obvious that Bentley, though the older member of a bungling warehouse burglary team, was a simple-minded man completely dominated by gun-freak Craig. Family petitions to the Queen were unsuccessful and Home Secretary Maxwell-Fyfe's rejection of the MPs' clemency call ended any hopes they had of a reprieve.

# Tito Elected Yugoslav President

Josip Tito, the Communist partisan leader whose Yugoslav guerrilla forces pinned down 12 Nazi armoured divisions in World War II and has maintained his political break from the dominance of Stalin's USSR regime since 1948, was today elected his country's president.

It is the climax of the long and colourful career of a man known to enjoy the company of beautiful women, fishing, dogs, diamonds, food and drink, and elaborate uniforms. A one-time soldier in the Austro-Hungarian army, Tito was an organizer for the Comintern before assuming command of Yugoslavia's partisans.

Pledging to continue his policy of non-alignment with either the Soviet bloc or the West, Tito proved his flexibility on January 8 by agreeing to meet Catholic bishops and discuss relations between the state and the church.

## NEWS IN BRIEF

**1:** Chinese leader Mao Tse-Tung announced his first five-year plan of new industrial and agricultural targets

**10:** Convicted spies Julius and Ethel Rosenberg, sentenced to death in April 1951, appealed to new US President Eisenhower for clemency

**22:** In London, BOAC grounded all of its Stratocruiser airliners after checks found an engine fault

## ARRIVALS
Born this month
**11:** John Sessions, British comic actor

## DEPARTURES
Died this month
**1:** Hank Williams (Hiram King Williams), US country singer/songwriter *(see Came & Went pages)*

# 128 Die In Irish Ferry Disaster

Only 44 passengers and crew survived when the cargo doors of a British Rail car ferry, *The Princess Victoria,* opened as she entered the sea off the Scottish port of Stranraer today. A total of 128 others, including skipper Captain James Ferguson, died as mountainous storm-driven waves flooded in to capsize the 2,694-ton boat.

The death toll was high because *The Princess Victoria* drifted away from its SOS position and sank off Belfast Lough, Ulster before a destroyer, *HMS Rothesay,* arrived to help. The ferry did not have a radio capable of sending a call to other craft, only a ship-to-shore link.

There was immediate criticism of the ferry's design and safety equipment. Many of the bodies recovered were wearing life jackets, but they had been forced to jump overboard and try to reach liferafts instead of leaving in lifeboats.

At an inquest held in February, a surviving crewman confirmed that a rear cargo door had still been open when *The Princess Victoria* set sail. No attempt to pump the water out could be made, said 44 year-old cargo handler Thomas McQuiston.

# Ike Sworn In

Dwight D. Eisenhower, former Allied Supreme Commander, mastermind of the Normandy landings and the final push against the Nazis, was inaugurated as President of the United States in Washington today (pictured right).

The ex-general, who scored a landslide election victory for the Republicans in November 1952, took the oath of office watched by his wife Mamie, Vice-President Richard Nixon and his wife Pat.

Ten days later Ike (as he is popularly known) used his military experience to order the US 7th Fleet to leave the Chinese island of Formosa, so allowing the Nationalist Chinese of Chiang Kai-shek to attack the Communist mainland regime of Mao Tse-Tung.

# Soviets Arrest Jewish Doctors

In what many observers believe is the start of a new anti-semitic purge by dictator Josef Stalin, Soviet security men today arrested nine distinguished Kremlin hospital doctors - six of them Jewish - and accused them of plotting to kill military and political leaders.

Allegations made against the doctors include the murder of party leaders and attempts to kill several military chiefs and so weaken Russia's defenses. According to police, the Jewish doctors took their orders from Western intelligence agencies and Zionist groups.

# Kenyan Whites March Against Mau Mau

**MORE THAN A THOUSAND** white Kenyan settlers marched through Nairobi to Government House today to call on the Governor of Kenya, Sir Evelyn Baring, to give them a bigger say in the country's administration and demand tougher action against the terrorist Mau Mau organization.

The march followed the murder of a white farmer, his wife and son, in the latest outrage by independence-seeking guerrillas. Drawn mainly from the highland Kikuyu tribe and led by Jomo Kenyatta - like thousands of his followers a British prisoner since November 1952 - the Mau Mau has been actively terrorizing settlers and non-member Kenyans for the past year.

Although Sir Evelyn refused to see the protestors, he announced the imminent arrival of Major-General William Hinde, the former deputy military governor of Berlin, to supervise new sweeps of the Aberdare Mountains, suspected hide-out of many young Mau Mau. Attacks on white farms continue despite the actions of vigilante commando units using Samburu tribal trackers.

The mood of white settlers was exemplified by one speaker at a protest meeting who called for the execution of 50,000 Kikuyu, and the publication of a newspaper article by Kenya-born author Elspeth Huxley, comparing Kenyatta with Adolf Hitler.

# UK Dentists Rejoice

**British dentists undoubtedly gave a secret shout of joy today as sweet rationing, introduced during World War II as sugar supplies dwindled, was finally lifted.**

Confectionery manufacturers can once more purchase cane-derived sugars for their creations, many of which vanished during the war and some of which were made using the less-satisfactory sugar-beet alternative or the chemically-created saccharine.

As British kids again enjoy unlimited access to delicious but dentally-challenging goodies, family dentists can anticipate an increase in calls for fillings and extractions.

# Floods Devastate English And Dutch Coastlines

**AT LEAST 283 PEOPLE** were drowned, thousands more made homeless and damage estimated at around £40 million ($120m) was caused along the east coast of England as hurricane winds combined with high tides to destroy sea defences from Lincolnshire to Kent.

A huge rescue operation was launched to reach hundreds of people trapped on rooftops. The Essex area of Canvey Island was worst hit, with 125 drowned and more than 500 missing. In the nearby resort of Clacton, holiday chalets were submerged in 12 feet of water and home owners were reported falling exhausted from rooftops.

Fatalities were also heavy in the low-lying county of Norfolk where 12 American servicemen in the Hunstanton airbase were among the 60 known to have drowned as an eight-foot wall of water raced inland to engulf villages more than five miles from the sea.

In Suffolk, rowing boats were used to reach and rescue 40 children trapped in a church, while the towns of Sutton-on-Sea and Mablethorpe were evacuated as hundreds more were left stranded.

The disaster was the second to hit mainland Britain this winter. In January, storms destroyed more than £3 million ($9m) worth of plantation trees owned by the Forestry Commission.

Across the North Sea, the same freak combination of conditions wreaked havoc on Holland, a country with vast tracts of reclaimed land lying beneath sea-level behind a series of dykes.

On February 3, more than 1,000 were reported killed when many miles of dykes were overwhelmed by storm-driven waves. The financial cost was also greater than Britain's as emergency repairs to the man-made barriers had to be quickly followed by more permanent re-building and reinforcement, with the eventual reclamation of vital land a priority.

# USSR Denies Judaism

In a move which uncannily matches the re-writing of history and historical facts depicted in George Orwell's prophetic novel 1984, a new encyclopedia published in Moscow today completely denied any claims made by or on behalf of the world's Jewish population.

With a double-think logic remarkable even for the Soviet propaganda machine, the encyclopedia managed to say both that the Jews are neither a nation nor a definable people, while describing Zionists (by definition Jews) as merely 'imperialist agents'!

# NEWS IN BRIEF

**5:** A record £250,000 ($750,000) was paid by an Irish stud for the Aga Khan's Tulyar, winner of the 1952 Derby

**11:** In Washington, President Eisenhower turned down the clemency appeal of Julius and Ethel Rosenberg

**12:** British magistrates voted for the restoration of corporal punishment

**16:** The British navy's new aircraft carrier, *HMS Hermes,* launched at Barrow, Cumberland

**27:** In the House of Commons, MPs gave a second reading to a private bill to simplify English spelling

**28:** The Hungarian government offered to exchange British cold-war prisoners gaoled for spying

**Born this month:**

**14:** Johannes 'Hans' Kranki, Austrian soccer star

**15:** Derek Conway, UK politician

## DEPARTURES

**Died this month:**

**24:** Gert von Runstedt, German commander during the 1944-45 Battle of The Bulge, dismissed by Hitler when outnumbered Allied troops defeated his armoured divisions. Aged 78.

---

## FEBRUARY 18

# Furore As French Reprieve Atrocity Collaborators

**THE FRENCH NATIONAL ASSEMBLY** was condemned internationally today for its decision to pardon 11 Frenchmen found guilty of complicity in the massacre of almost 700 inhabitants of the village of Oradour-sur-Glane by SS troops in 1944.

The obliteration of the village, some 16 miles from Limoges, was a Nazi reprisal for the killing of an SS officer. Only seven people survived when menfolk were taken in groups of 20 and shot in a barn, after which women and children were locked in a church which was set ablaze with a box of explosives set on the altar. Any who managed to scramble through windows were shot by soldiers surrounding the building.

A total of 25 ex-SS men and 11 French collaborators stood in the dock of a Bordeaux courtroom when their trial opened on January 12. All defendants were found guilty when the jury returned their verdict on February 13, and all were either sentenced to death or given long prison sentences.

The National Assembly's pardon of the Frenchmen is seen by many commentators as proof of the French establishment's continued reluctance to confront the reality of widespread complicity with the wartime Vichy government, many members of which remain in positions of political authority at a national and local level.

---

## FEBRUARY 5

## Rhodesia Plans Announced

If British government plans announced in London today go through, a new African state of more than 7 million will be created. While the interests of black Africans in the new country are said to be paramount, the government has dismissed African critics as 'unrepresentative'.

With its legislative authorities based in the Southern Rhodesian capital, Salisbury, the new Federation is designed to mix and balance the mining and labour resources of the protectorates with the richness of the white Rhodesian farming communities.

---

## FEBRUARY 1

## Wider Still And Wider

In a move described as the biggest to impact on the film world since the introduction of sound in 1927, Hollywood giant 20th Century Fox today announced plans to convert its entire movie production to the new wide-screen format, Cinemascope.

The studio is to invest $25 million (£8m) in major Cinemascope productions, with veteran director Cecil B. DeMille's biblical epic *The Robe* slated to begin first.

Aware of increased and continued rivalry from television, Fox executives hope the new system, which employs a special lens to project films onto a 145-degree curved screen, will pull audiences back to movie houses worldwide. The new format will be enhanced by the use of the more life-like stereophonic sound.

**FEB**

# Brain Haemorrhage Kills Stalin - Khrushchev Moves In

**ONLY FOUR DAYS AFTER** suffering a massive cerebral haemorrhage which left him speechless and largely unconscious, 73 year old Soviet leader Josef Stalin died in Moscow today to end a 30-year reign of brutality matched in this century only by that of Adolf Hitler.

The four-day gap was used by Communist Party leaders to begin a behind-the-scenes carve-up of top jobs and plan how they would orchestrate official mourning. While many ordinary Soviet citizens will grieve their leader's passing, millions more will breathe sighs of relief and pray for a less vicious regime. These include the countless thousands locked away in the remote prison camps of Stalin's notorious gulag archipelago.

Almost single-handedly responsible for creating the USSR, Stalin - born Josef Vissarionovich Djugashvili - proved a superb military leader during WWII. His paranoia about real and imagined rivals led to the terrible extremes future leaders would reveal.

Stalin's successor proved to be Nikita Khrushchev, the 59 year old given responsibility for organizing the dead dictator's funeral.

As the body lay in state in the old Nobleman's Club, scene of the mock trial Stalin staged to justify his eventual execution of Bolshevik rivals when he first came to power, Khrushchev saw off the challenge of Georgi Malenkov, both Prime Minister and First Secretary of the Communist party. While Malenkov became the USSR's nominal leader by retaining the premiership, Khrushchev's gain of the key party post in September made him the real power in the land.

By becoming head of the all-powerful party secretariat and the ruling Politburo, Khrushchev was

## ARRIVALS

**Born this month:**

**3:** Zico (Artur Antunes Coimbra), Brazilian soccer star

## DEPARTURES

**Died this month:**

**5:** Josef Stalin, Soviet dictator *(see lead story)*; Sergei Prokofiev, Russian composer

**7:** Herman J. Mankiewicz, Oscar-winning US screenwriter *(Citizen Kane)*

**23:** Raoul Dufy, French painter *(see Came & Went pages)*

**25:** Queen Mary of England *(see story)*

**28:** Jim Thorpe, US athlete *(see story)*

able to pack the party at will. His passage to power was helped by the disappearance of Stalin's personal aide, General Poskrebychev, the reduction of the Politburo's membership from 36 to 14, and the sacking of five Secretariat members.

A fascinating mixture of secret guile, driving ambition and public affability, the humbly-born and formally little-educated Khrushchev joined the Communist party in 1918 and became a Politburo member in 1939. A trusted Stalin aide, he supervised purges which eradicated opposition to the dictator's regime in the Ukraine.

## Queen Mary Dies

Queen Mary, the Queen's grandmother and widow of King George V, died in her sleep at her London home, Marlborough House, it was announced by Buckingham Palace today.

A reclusive person for the last years of her life, Queen Mary was 86.

Bearing the title Princess Mary of Teck before her marriage to King George, she had developed a personal and distinctive dress style which she maintained for 50 years - tightly-packed curls topped with jewelled toques, the same-style coat and an unchanging silver-topped walking cane. Queen Mary was buried alongside her husband in the royal family's chapel at Windsor Castle on March 31.

# NEWS IN BRIEF

**2:** A record 5,000 East Germans are listed as seeking asylum in the West

**5:** In Cambodia, King Norodom Sihanouk proclaimed his country's independence

**10:** The West German government banned the neo-Nazi movement, Freikorps Deutschland

**20:** Actress Vivien Leigh returned to London from Hollywood, suffering an acute nervous breakdown

**28:** The Grand National at Aintree Racecourse, Liverpool, was won by Early Mist

---

# Salk Tests Polio Vaccine

American medical pioneer Dr. Jonas Salk today revealed that he had carried out apparently-successful tests on an anti-polio vaccine, offering hope of an answer to a disease which kills many young people and leaves survivors with permanently wasted legs.

According to Dr. Salk, the level of antibodies in the 161 adults and children who took part in the trials had remained steady for more than four months. While this was encouraging, he and his team were still some way off creating a practical vaccine for widespread use.

---

MARCH 31

# New UN Head

Swedish diplomat Dag Hammerskjöld, 48, was today elected the new Secretary-General of the United Nations, succeeding Norwegian Trygve Lie who had held the post since the UN's inaugural 1946 session in London.

A gifted and dogged negotiator, Hammerskjöld would successfully encourage increased and active UN intervention to preserve world peace. He would personally persuade Egyptian President Nasser to accept a UN peace force which would hold the Middle East peace-line for 10 years.

---

MARCH 28

# Fallen Hero Jim Thorpe Dies

American athlete Jim Thorpe - double hero of the 1912 Stockholm Olympic Games when he won Gold for both the pentathlon and decathlon, but stripped of all titles and record-book entries a year later when he admitted having played minor league baseball for $25 a week - died today at the age of 64.

Thorpe's achievements were all the more remarkable because of his American Indian ancestry, at that time a severe handicap in most areas of public life. A top-class college footballer before being spotted for his greater athletics potential, Thorpe admitted to playing baseball in North Carolina in the 1909-10 season, so making him ineligible for the strictly amateur Olympics.

---

MARCH 29

# Tito Extends Hand

President Tito began his new life as Yugoslavia's supremo with two gestures designed to confirm his reputation as one communist leader the rest of the world can at least approach.

On March 1, the Turkish city of Ankara was the scene for the signing of an historic friendship treaty between Yugoslavia, Greece and Turkey. While the Greeks and Turks would continue to find new excuses to not maintain this amity, both countries would honour the friendship with Yugoslavia.

Tito also became the first communist head of state to visit Britain on March 15, when he began a trip which included talks with Prime Minister Winston Churchill, a wartime ally against Hitler's Germany despite their vastly different political beliefs.

# Serial Killer Christie Caught

**A GIGANTIC** nationwide manhunt ended today with the arrest of John Christie, sought by police since the remains of three women - one of them his wife Ethel - were discovered by a man installing a bathroom in his recently vacated London home on March 25.

The terraced house, in the quiet Notting Hill cul-de-sac of Rillington Place, was already notorious. In 1949 it was the scene of the double murder of Mrs Beryl Evans and her infant daughter Geraldine - killings for which Timothy John Evans had been convicted and hanged, despite his protestations of innocence.

Christie, who also lived at No. 10 with his wife, had been a key prosecution witness at Evans' trial. During their intensive search of the house after the new grisly discoveries, police found a newspaper clipping about the Evans case which Christie had stowed away.

MAR

# FROM HERE TO ETERNITY IN OSCARS SMASH AND GRAB RAID

**T**he competition for 1953's Academy Awards made the annual ceremony a real nail-biter as a number of exceptional movies and brilliant actors vied for coveted trophies. The final nominations for Best Picture included Fred Zinneman's eve-of-war epic *From Here To Eternity,* William Wyler's witty comedy *Roman Holiday,* the first widescreen CinemaScope biblical epic *The Robe,* Joseph L.Mankiewicz's US-UK production of *Julius Caesar* and George Stevens' haunting western *Shane.* A formidable clutch of contestants.

It didn't end there. Although not listed in the top category, the Leslie Caron musical *Lili* won nominations for Caron and director Charles Walters, while the WWII prison camp drama *Stalag 17* gained director William Wyler and star William Holden well-deserved nominations.

In the event, *From Here To Eternity* was the flick which swept pretty well all before it, winning the Best Picture award, giving director Zinneman his second

Oscar, giving Frank Sinatra his dues as Best Supporting Actor and Donna Reed hers as Best Supporting Actress.

Daniel Taradash's screenplay was judged worthy of an Oscar, while Burnett Guffy's photography and William Lyon's skills won them the best black-and-white cinematography and editing prizes.

A measure of the film's quality in depth can be established by the fact that Burt Lancaster and Montgomery Clift were unsuccessful nominees for the Best Actor award and Deborah Kerr came equally close in the Best Actress category which was won by the elfin Audrey Hepburn's performance in *Roman Holiday.*

**I**t was a case of third time unlucky for Marlon Brando. Nominated unsuccessfully for the Best Actor award in 1951 (for *A Streetcar Named Desire*) and 1952 (for *Viva Zapata!*), he lucked out again this year with *Julius Caesar,* a film many thought should have won James Mason at least a

**From Here to Eternity:**
**dominated the Oscars**

nomination for his powerful and devious Brutus.

Nominated as Best Supporting Actor in 1952 for *My Cousin Rachel*, screen relative newcomer Richard Burton's ascendancy was confirmed by his Best Actor nomination this year for *The Robe*, though the omission of a best-performance-yet from Victor Mature in the same movie confused his legion of fans.

The absence of leading man Alan Ladd from the nominations was equally baffling, though no-one begrudged fellow-*Shane* players Brandon De Wilde and Jack Palance their Best Supporting Actor nominations.

And while the world's record-buyers don't always agree with the Best Original Song award, they did this year as *Secret Love* became an international smash for Doris Day, star of *Calamity Jane*, another otherwise un-nominated box office hit.

APRIL

# DNA Structure Revealed?

Two Cambridge-based molecular biologists - American James D. Watson and Englishman Francis Crick - appear to have solved one of the greatest scientific mysteries: how living organisms reproduce themselves.

In a paper published today in the journal *Nature*, the two propose a structure for the chemical deoxyribonucleic acid (or DNA), the core material of genes through which hereditary characteristics are passed from parents to offspring.

Extending research completed in London by New Zealander Maurice Wilkins and his colleague Rosalind Franklin, Crick and Watson's DNA structure consists of two strands of complementary elements which fit together in a 'key' double helix which, when uncoiled, links perfectly with other 'keys' to create two identical copies of the original.

The breakthrough would win Watson and Crick the 1962 Nobel Prize for Medicine, but not for the unjustly overlooked Franklin.

# 'Burning Spear' Kenyatta Sentenced

JOMO 'BURNING SPEAR' Kenyatta (pictured right) was sentenced to seven years hard labour today after a Kenyan court found him guilty of master-minding the pro-independence Mau Mau movement responsible for the murder of white settlers and the widespread terrorizing of Africans not supporting their aims.

Five other leading Mau Mau figures, held with Kenyatta in the remote Kapenguria government station since November 1952, were given identical sentences.

Addressing the paraffin-lit court as a lightning storm raged biblically outside, Kenyatta protested the innocence of all accused and said their prosecution was a political act designed to crush the fight for African people's rights.

He and the Mau Mau were not anti-white, he claimed, but they were determined to see black Africans govern their own country.

# Ike Meets Adenauer

An historic moment in Washington today when President Eisenhower, one of the principal architects of the defeat of German dictator Adolf Hitler, welcomed West German Chancellor Konrad Adenauer - a noted anti-Nazi who spent WWII in exile - to the White House.

The summit will prove invaluable to Adenauer as he continues to bury his nation's inglorious past, rebuild a country shattered by the war, and establish West Germany's role as a dynamic member of the post-war international community.

# Mau Mau Hunt Builds

Kenya's crackdown on the Mau Mau terrorist organization continued to build this month. With the movement's leader Jomo Kenyatta beginning a seven-year prison sentence, on March 1 British troops claimed an overwhelming victory when they killed 24 Mau Mau guerrillas and captured 36 others in a swoop raid. On March 17 another massive operation resulted in the arrest of more than a thousand suspected Mau Mau near Nairobi.

## ARRIVALS

Born this month:
**10:** David Moorcroft, British Olympic athlete, now TV commentator. Set world record of 13 mins 00.41 secs for the 5,000 metres at Oslo meeting in July 1982
**30:** Merrill Osmond, US singer (The Osmonds)

## DEPARTURES

Died this month:
**2:** Jean Epstein, French film director, author
**4:** King Carol II, ex-ruler of Romania between 1930-1940

## USSR Doctors Released

A unique U-turn today in Moscow saw the release of the nine Russian doctors arrested in January on charges of plotting or attempting to kill leading government and military figures.

Admitting that they had been falsely accused and arrested, a spokesman for the new government said the nine - six of them Jewish - had all been tortured on the orders of the now-dead dictator Stalin to ensure phony confessions.

# Charlie Chaplin Driven From US

A resident of America for the past 40 years, during which time he became one of the world's best-loved and most successful movie stars, Charlie Chaplin today announced he will never return there.

Victim of the increasingly-virulent anti-communist witch-hunt being carried out by Senator Joe McCarthy, chairman of the US House Committee on Un-American Activities, Chaplin is only the most recent and best-known Hollywood figure to be drawn into the Wisconsin politician's net.

Like many others, the comic genius chose not to expose himself to McCarthy's aggressive and unpleasant questioning, but had confined his defence to press statements. Found guilty in his absence, Chaplin had left Hollywood to promote his new movie *Limelight* and been warned of proceedings to bar him as a 'dangerous alien' if he tried to return.

Speaking from the new home in Vevey, Switzerland, in which he, his wife Oona (pictured right with children Michael and Geraldine) and their four children have settled, the 64 year old said he'd surrendered his re-entry permit. 'I have been the object of vicious propaganda', he added.

# UN And N. Koreans Swap Prisoners

**AS FIGHTING CONTINUED** a matter of miles away, Allied and Communist wounded and sick prisoners were exchanged at Panmunjon, Korea, today - some of the first to be swapped in carefully-negotiated deals.

Many of the 100 UN prisoners were returned wearing the distinctive blue padded uniforms of their Chinese captors - the first thing they wanted to discard on arrival at the newly-built 'Freedom Village' in nearby Munsan, where they were given toiletries, chocolates and cigarettes by Red Cross workers.

Also on hand to help de-brief the men were officers specially trained to identify and counsel those suspected of having been brainwashed or indoctrinated by the Chinese, a practice known to be widespread in prison camps from which the prisoners have been released.

But the greatest priority is to get them home, as soon as their physical injuries permit.

# Mystery Of BOAC Comet Crash

**AN EMERGENCY ENQUIRY** was ordered today following the mysterious crash near Calcutta, India of a Comet jet airliner, new flagship of the British Overseas Airways Corporation fleet.

All 43 passengers and crew were killed as the jet crashed into a dry streambead during a storm. An eye-witness reported seeing a bright red flash and what seemed to be a wingless plane flying low over trees. After several more explosions, the Comet dived into the riverbed.

While an early theory suggests the airliner may have been hit by a high-velocity wind-squall, official investigators will have to discover why the Comet lost its wings.

## MAY 18

# Police Exhume Evans Bodies

London police today exhumed the bodies of Beryl Evans and her infant daughter Geraldine as enquiries continued into the case of John Christie, arrested in March and now charged with the murder of four women in the same house he and his wife once shared with Timothy Evans, convicted and hanged for his wife and daughter's murders.

The exhumation comes as calls for a complete review of the Evans case begin to build.

# Brits Quit Egypt

Advised by Foreign Office officials that their safety could not be guaranteed, British families began to leave Egypt today.

The local situation has deteriorated badly since the most recent set of talks between Britain and Egypt to settle the future of the Suez Canal Zone reach stalemate.

It is clear that the military government of President Neguib, which seized power from the now-exiled King Farouk in July 1952, is poised to force Britain to return control of the Suez Canal to Egypt, lost in October 1951 when British troops launched a surprise dawn invasion to take key positions around the strategic waterway.

## Pulitzer For Hemingway

American novelist, big-game hunter and bullfighting buff Ernest Hemingway was awarded a coveted Pulitzer Prize in New York today.

The works for which he won his award were *The Old Man And The Sea* and *Picnic*.

A combatant and war correspondent during the Spanish Civil War in the 1930s, Hemingway would win the Nobel Prize for Literature in 1954, and shoot himself in 1961 when his health failed.

## Starving Refugees Flood West Berlin

The exodus of refugees to West Berlin from the Russian-controlled sector of Germany increased dramatically today as more than 2,000 hungry East Germans risked being shot by border guards to find sanctuary and food.

The rush was initiated by the sudden withdrawal of ration cards from the 2 million who live near the border. Food shortages are known to be bad in the East, but Communist authorities there have rejected Western offers to send £4 million ($12m) worth of relief supplies to help.

## Dulles Warns Of Far-East 'Domino Effect'

The worsening situation in Indo-China, where North Vietnamese Viet Minh guerrillas have scored a number of notable victories over French forces, led to US Secretary of State John Foster Dulles warning the international community today that the whole of south-east Asia could fall, 'just like a row of dominoes', if the Communists drive France out.

The first-known use of what will become a popular phrase came as it was learned that the Viet Minh army of Ho Chi Minh has established control over a small area of neighbouring Siam. From there they could launch fresh assaults on French troops now led by General Henri Navarre.

## ARRIVALS

**Born this month:**

**6:** Graeme Souness, Scottish football star

**19:** Victoria Wood, UK comedienne, actress and writer

**22:** Paul Mariner, English football star

**26:** Daniel Passarella, Argentinian football star

## DEPARTURES

**Died this month:**

**26:** 'Django' Reinhardt (Jean-Baptiste), Belgian-born gypsy jazz guitarist *(see Came & Went pages)*

**MAY 8**

# Heroes Welcomes For Returning PoWs

**THE PEOPLE OF THE US AND BRITAIN** joined in celebration this month with the families of UN servicemen released from North Korean prison camps in PoW exchanges which began on April 20.

Typical of the welcome ceremonies was that held at RAF Lyneham, Wiltshire on May 1 to greet 22 British heroes after a seven-day, 10,000-mile trip from Panmunjon. The men, four of whom were carried on stretchers, were swamped by a large crowd of cheering and weeping relatives, friends and colleagues as they finally reached home soil.

Some of those returning were survivors of the Gloucestershire Regiment's historic stand against overwhelming odds at the 1951 Battle of Imjin River when troops led by Lieutenant Colonel Carne beat back a huge Chinese force.

Held in prison since then, all wore the distinctive blue flash of the American Presidential Citation which they had just been awarded.

**MAY 2**

## 'Dribble Wizard' Matthews Wins First FA Cup

Although the north London soccer giants Arsenal captured British sports headlines on May 1 when they secured the English League Championship for a record seventh time, today's front pages were devoted to Stanley Matthews (pictured right), the 38 year old 'wizard of dribble' who helped Blackpool win the most thrilling FA Cup Final ever held at Wembley Stadium. The veteran winger, rated as one of the world's most exciting and inventive soccer players of all time, must have thought that a cup winner's medal – one of the few prizes to have evaded him in a long club and international career – was lost when his side's opponents, Bolton Wanderers, led 3-1 with less than 30 minutes to play.

A pin-point pass to striker Stan Mortenson from Matthews split the Bolton defense and allowed Mortenson to pull a goal back, and then equalize with a rocketing free kick only two minutes from time. With only a minute left, Matthews once more baffled his opposing full-back, crossed into the goalmouth and joined celebrations as Bill Perry shot the winning goal.

JUNE

## Soviets Crush Berlin Workers' Revolt

Russian tanks and troop carriers filled East Berlin today to crush a two-day uprising of workers which followed an East German government order for construction workers on a Stalin Allee project to increase output by 10 per cent.

Even today it is not clear exactly how many died in the anti-Soviet riots and their aftermath, but hundreds were injured and buildings used by Soviet officials set ablaze despite a declaration of martial law and a 9pm-5am curfew by the Soviet commandant Major General P.T. Dibrowa, as a crowd of over 100,000 besieged government buildings in the Wilhelmstrasse.

The arrival of Soviet reinforcements soon put a bloody end to the workers' revolt. It would also end the career of the East German minister for state security, who was fired in July.

# Elizabeth Crowned In Pomp And Ceremony

**WITH ALL THE PAGEANTRY** born of a thousand years of tradition, the coronation of Queen Elizabeth II was held at Westminster Abbey today, watched for the first time by millions around the world as the BBC transmitted live coverage of the event.

The ceremony, held in an Abbey packed with monarchs, ministers, peers and VIPs from all quarters of the globe, saw the new Queen swear to serve the people of Britain and the Commonwealth as Dr. Fisher, the Archbishop of Canterbury, placed the Coronation crown on her head and she took the ceremonial mace and sceptre - symbols of her powers - in her hands.

With the Queen, and first after Dr. Fisher to place his hands between hers in an act of homage, was the Duke of Edinburgh. Earlier, he had followed the Queen's Golden Coach as it travelled from Buckingham Palace, cheered wildly by vast crowds who stoically ignored the cold, wet weather.

While there were enough carriages to carry all the dignitaries, a shortage of coachmen meant many of the coaches in processions to and from the Abbey were driven by horsey millionaires and country gents who'd volunteered to dress up and play at being flunkeys for the day.

The day came to a dramatic climax at midnight when, after a still-cheering throng had greeted the Queen and Duke who appeared on a Buckingham Palace balcony, the skies over the River Thames were filled with a fireworks display as spectacular as the ceremony it celebrated.

## ARRIVALS

Born this month:
**2:** Dave 'Boy' Green, British professional boxer
**5:** Julian Hosking, principal dancer, Royal Ballet
**20:** Paul Ramirez, tennis player

## DEPARTURES

Died this month:
**8:** Sir Godfrey Seymour Tearle, British actor
**9:** Ugo Betti, Italian playwright and judge
**16:** Margaret Bondfield, British socialist politician, first woman cabinet minister, 1929
**19:** Julius and Ethel Rosenberg, US spies for USSR *(see story)*

## Rosenbergs Die In Electric Chair

With all avenues for clemency closed to them, including a rejected appeal to President Eisenhower, convicted spies Julius and Ethel Rosenberg were executed in the Sing Sing prison electric chair this evening.

Sentenced to death in 1951 as the witch-hunt mounted by Senator Joe McCarthy was at its height, the Rosenbergs are the first married couple in America to be executed together, and the first to die for espionage.

A crowd of 5,000 held vigil in Union Square, New York to protest Eisenhower's refusal of a pardon to a couple who, observers said, displayed 'quiet dignity' in the moments before they each received a 2,000 volt charge to end their lives.

# Christie To Hang

Found guilty of murdering four women, including his wife Ethel, John Christie was today sentenced to death.

The London jury had dismissed the balding, bespectacled transport clerk's plea of insanity after hearing evidence that Christie, a special constable with the Metropolitan Police, had attempted intercourse with his three prostitute victims after using coal gas to render them unconscious.

All four had been strangled. The body of his wife was hidden beneath floorboards, the others were hidden behind a false wall.

Christie told police of three other killings, including those of Mrs Beryl Evans and her baby daughter, for which Timothy Evans had been hanged in 1950 after a trial in which Christie had been a key witness.

## Chinese Attack In Korea

Only weeks before the date set for the official armistice ceremony to end the Korean War, 30,000 Chinese troops launched a surprise offensive on Allied positions today, meeting the American Third Infantry Division and two South Korean divisions along a 30-mile front.

Experts believed the attack was no more than a bizarre propaganda exercise.

# Stroke Fells Churchill

The British Prime Minister today suffered a severe stroke which partially paralyzed his left side and temporarily left him unable to speak. Doctors were rushed to his official residence at 10 Downing Street and only a few cabinet members were told the truth about his collapse.

While some newspapers learned the facts, all cooperated with a news blackout initiated by Lord Beaverbrook, owner of the Daily Express group and a long-time confidant of the 79 year old premier.

It would be four days before a bulletin announced Churchill had been taken ill, needed complete rest and must lighten his duties 'for at least a month'.

# Hillary And Ten-Sing Conquer Everest

**MOUNT EVEREST,** the world's highest mountain and long the elusive target of international climbers, has been conquered, it was confirmed today in messages received from the Nepal capital Kathmandu.

History was actually made on May 29 when New Zealander Edmund Hillary and Norgay Ten-sing (pictured left), the Sherpa guide who'd accompanied him on the final climb, stood on the 29,002-foot peak. Members of a British Commonwealth team led by Colonel John Hunt, the two spent 15 minutes on what Hillary described as the 'symmetrical, beautiful snow-cone summit'. While there they took photographs of each other and ate celebratory mint cake before leaving a Union Jack, a Nepal national flag and a UN banner, along with traditional Buddhist offerings of sweets and biscuits.

The conquest followed an unsuccessful attempt earlier in May which was beaten by high winds. Hillary and Ten-sing enjoyed fine settled conditions, and benefited from the lightweight clothing and oxygen equipment specified by Colonel Hunt, who had made a detailed scientific study of all previous expeditions.

On July 16, Hillary and Hunt would be knighted by the Queen in London, while Ten-sing would receive the George Cross, Britain's highest award for civilian courage.

## SOCCER
## ARSENAL AND RANGERS SNEAK TITLES ON GOALS

A nail-biting 1952-53 season dominated by Stanley Matthews' sterling FA Cup Final at Wembley *(see News Pages)*, saw Arsenal and Glasgow Rangers shave the English and Scottish First Division titles by goal difference.

Arsenal's championship was at the expense of Preston North End, while Rangers shaved it over Hibernian - a reversal of the previous season's championship race. Rangers also took the Scottish FA Cup, beating Aberdeen 1-0 in a replay forced by a first-go 1-1 draw.

## MOTOR RACING
## ASCARI WORLD CHAMP, HAWTHORN WINS FIRST GP, HEAT AND DEATHS MAR INDY 500

Alberto Ascari's victories in the Argentinian, Dutch, Belgian, British and Swiss Grands Prix ensured him victory over Juan Fangio and Guiseppe Farina in the World Drivers' Championship in a season which included the first-ever GP win by a British driver - Mike Hawthorn's at Rheims, France.

But the motor world's attentions were focused on the United States.

Always a dangerous event, the 37th Indianapolis 500 was held in a heatwave which saw trackside temperatures soar to an incredible 130°F (54°C), drivers drop out with heat exhaustion, and two of America's best drivers die.

Warning signs came during qualifying when Chet Miller, who'd set a track record of almost 139 mph in 1952, was killed in the contest to win pole position.

That was won by Bill Vukovich, whose Kurtis-Offy 500A's time was only tenths of a second outside Miller's record.

Vukovich stamped his superiority on the race from word go, building up a nine second lead by lap three. Incidents began to mount during lap 4. Andy Linden somehow escaped unhurt when his car burst into flames after hitting a wall and brake-loss forced Jim Davies to use the pit stop wall as his only way of slowing down.

During lap 76, the steering arm of Bob Freeland's Watson-Offy snapped and he too ploughed into a wall. Meanwhile, the combination of heat and nitromethane fuel fumes forced the substitution of a number of drivers, among them Cale Yarborough, who collapsed as he climbed from his car. Rushed to hospital, he died.

Vukovich piled on the pressure, losing the lead for only five laps during his three pit-stops when his crew poured ice-cold water down his shirt. He went on to win with three laps in hand, recording a victory which also heralded a new era at Indianapolis. The roadster had arrived.

## GOLF
## HOGAN'S ROLL CONTINUES

The supremacy of Ben Hogan was reinforced this year as the American swept to victory in the British Open, the US Masters and the US Open. His complete dominance was averted only by missing the US PGA - it clashed with the British Open. That was won by Walter Burkemo, who staged a phenomenal late run after being seven holes adrift at lunch.

Hogan's US Masters win - the second time he'd donned the green blazer - also saw him set a 14-under Augusta record.

As ever, the USA strolled through the Ryder Cup match against Britain and Ireland at Wentworth, winning it 6-5, with one game halved.

## AMERICAN FOOTBALL
### LIONS' LAYNE IS COME-BACK KING

At Detroit's Biggs Stadium, the Cleveland Browns - NFL champions with an 11-1 season - were determined to avenge their 17-7 defeat in the 1952 championship final by the team they faced once again, the AFC's Detroit Lions.

It seems no-one had shown Detroit quarterback Bobby Layne the script. In a final quarter revival, he hauled his team back from 16-10 down with a march from his own 20 yard line, using substitute end Jim Doran as his main receiver - and it was Doran who caught the 33-yard touchdown pass Layne hurled to tie the score.

It all rested on kicker Doak Walker, and it's said that people in Toronto heard the roar which greeted his successful conversion to make Detroit the 1953 champions and establish Bobby Layne in legend as The Comeback King.

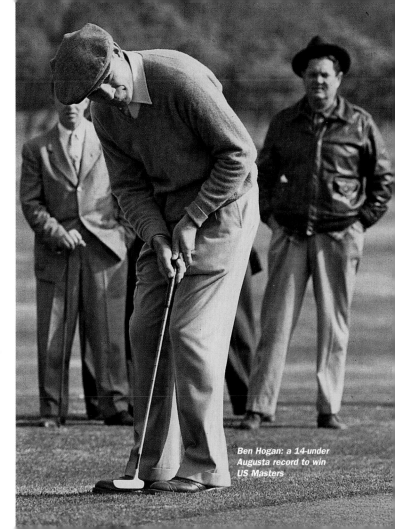

*Ben Hogan: a 14-under Augusta record to win US Masters*

JULY

## Soviets Arrest Police Chief Beria

Lavrenti Beria, Stalin's secret police chief since 1941 and one of Soviet Russia's most feared men, has been arrested and charged with being a Western agent and plotting to seize power, it was confirmed today.

Second in the Soviet hierarchy after Prime Minister Georgi Malenkov, Beria was arrested at a Politburo meeting called last month to demand his resignation. Acting on a signal from Malenkov, armed marshals seized the man whose secret police systematically arrested, tortured or eliminated countless thousands of people Stalin suspected of opposing his regime.

Beria's fall has been quickly followed by a purge of the secret police, though no-one believes a change of leadership there will result in more benign conduct by Russia's new political masters.

# Evans Was Guilty, Inquiry Rules

**TIMOTHY EVANS,** whose responsibility for the 1949 murder of his wife and daughter was thrown into doubt by the conviction last month of John Christie for four other murders at the same address, was guilty according to a government inquiry which released its findings today.

Despite a confession from Christie, who gave evidence to the tribunal led by John Scott Henderson, QC in his cell, the report expressed confidence that the Welsh-born truck driver did deserve to hang. Christie's confession was, it said, unreliable and untrue, and was made only to 'help his defence'.

The Howard League for Penal Reform, along with a number of Labour Party MPs, have refused to accept the report and have called for a full public debate of the case.

Christie, who refused to meet Labour MPs, was hanged in London on July 15, taking the truth with him and leaving the way clear for years of argument about who did what at 10 Rillington Place.

# Nagy Promises Hungarians New Deal

Hungary's new Prime Minister, Imre Nagy, unveiled plans today which would, if delivered, completely transform the Russian-dominated country.

Nagy has pledged to end the enforced collectivization of agriculture, allow the freedom to worship and travel, and to abolish internment camps.

Commentators are not sure Nagy's Russian masters will approve of such moves, nor his stated intention to begin trading with capitalist countries.

# Gentlemen Love Monroe And Russell

One of this year's biggest movie hits, the Marilyn Monroe-Jane Russell (pictured left) musical *Gentlemen Prefer Blondes,* had its New York première today.

Based on the Anita Loos comic novel about a gold-digging twenties chorus girl, the film won rave reviews for both stars and made an unlikely singing sensation out of Monroe. Her big number, *Diamonds Are A Girl's Best Friend,* would have stopped the show if it was a stage musical.

It's the second time the story's been told on-screen. The first version, starring Ruth Taylor and Alice White, was made in 1928.

## ARRIVALS

**Born this month:**
**5:** Elizabeth Emanuel, British dressmaker, designer, with husband David, made Princess Diana's wedding dress in 1981
**6:** Nanci Griffith, US folk-country singer, songwriter *(see Came & Went pages)*
**13:** Larry Gomes, West Indian cricket player
**23:** Graham Gooch, English cricket player, former national captain

## DEPARTURES

**Died this month:**
**12:** Joseph Jongen, Belgian composer
**15:** John Reginald Halliday Christie, British serial killer, hanged *(see main story)*
**16:** Hilaire Pierre Belloc, British poet, author

| JULY 27 |
| --- |

# Peace Breaks Out In Korea

**AFTER THREE YEARS** of vicious fighting estimated to have cost more than 2 million lives, the Korean War came to an official end today with the signing of an armistice at Panmunjon.

The truce stipulates that both sides will destroy and quit their front-line positions and withdraw two kilometres. Allied air and naval blockades will be lifted and troops occupying North Korean islands will pull out. A special committee will supervise the exchange of prisoners.

A key clause in the deal, which has taken two years to negotiate, stipulates that neither side will reinforce existing forces or increase supplies.

Allied Commander General Mark Clark was cautiously optimistic when facing world press this evening. 'It is good to have the bloodshed end', he said. 'But a long and difficult road lies ahead. There are no short cuts and we must continue our efforts to seek and defend peace'.

| JULY 1 |
| --- |

# MPs Reject Hanging 'Holiday'

A private bill to suspend the death penalty in Britain for five years was voted out in the House of Commons today.

The bill's timing could not have been worse. With public outrage at the Christie case running high and the government promising an inquiry into that of Timothy Evans, its chances of success were always slim.

## JULY 26

# Cubans Arrest Rebel Castro

Troops loyal to Cuban president Batista today repelled a Communist rebel attack on two army barracks near Santiago, killed 55 of the insurgents and captured their leader, Fidel Castro.

The lawyer son of a wealthy plantation owner, Castro was recently implicated in a coup attempt in the nearby Dominican Republic. Known to Cuban security chiefs for some time, the Jesuit-educated Castro was allegedly involved in a terrorist group while still a student, and his arrest is a blow to anti-Batista factions.

## JULY 4

# Second Wimbledon Win For Little Mo

American teenager Maureen 'Little Mo' Connolly won her second successive Wimbledon Championship today when the 17 year old beat her countrywoman Doris Hart 8-6, 7-5 in a hard match which had the capacity crowds on the edge of their seats.

Doris Hart had the consolation of a Ladies Doubles victory over Connolly when she and Joan Fry become three times in a row champs by beating Little Mo and Julia Sampson 6-0, 6-0.

The Men's title was won by American Victor Seixas, who beat Dane Kurt Nielsen 9-7, 6-3, 6-4. Seixas and Hart combined in the Mixed Doubles to win the first of their three successive titles.

# Soviet Union Claims It Has H-Bomb

**WESTERN LEADERS WERE SHOCKED** today when the Soviet Prime Minister, Georgi Malenkov, used a speech to a session of the Supreme Soviet - the Russian parliament - to announce that the Soviet Union has caught up with the United States in the nuclear arms race by developing its own hydrogen bomb.

Until now, only America has built H-bombs, the world's most powerful weapon. While Western scientists greeted Malenkov's claim with initial disbelief, saying that no nuclear explosions had been detected in the Soviets' Kazakhstan test site since 1951, they admitted that a Russian breakthrough was not impossible.

Malenkov used his Supreme Soviet speech to launch a bitter attack on US foreign policy, especially its Far East dealings, and made his H-bomb revelation almost as an afterthought.

It's not clear whether this is because the claim is untrue and a classic bluff or, if it is true, because Malenkov did not wish to give any credit to former secret police chief Lavrenti Beria, the man appointed by Stalin to oversee nuclear weapon development but now facing treason charges.

## From Here To Immortality

Destined to become one of the all-time movie classics, *From Here To Eternity* was screened for the first time in the US today. Based on James Jones' gritty anti-army novel which climaxed with the Japanese attack on Pearl Harbor, the Fred Zinneman-directed epic drew Oscar-winning performances from supporting stars Frank Sinatra and Donna Reed and nominations for Montgomery Clift, Burt Lancaster and Deborah Kerr (pictured below).
If anyone had awarded a Clinch of the Decade award, there's no doubt Kerr and Lancaster's torrid (for the time) beach party entwinings would have won hands down!

# Easterners Raid Western Foodstores

The widespread food shortages known to exist in East Germany led to one of the most bizarre smash-and-grab raids ever today, when 6,000 men and women from the East raided two food distribution centres in West Berlin.

It was certainly the strangest event yet in the often-incongruous history of the Cold War and could not have happened without the blessing of East German authorities, who have steadfastly refused all Western offers of food aid.

## ARRIVALS

**Born this month:**

**2:** Anne Leuchars, British TV journalist

**3:** Osvaldo Ardiles, Argentine international soccer player, British-based manager/coach

**8:** Nigel Mansell, British, World Formula One and US Indy motor racing champion

**24:** Sam Torrance, professional golfer

## AUGUST 19

# England Regain Ashes After Twenty Years

Celebrations by English cricket fans were unreserved today at the Oval ground in south London as the national team ended a 20-year spell as underdogs to Australia and finally won a Test match series to regain the Ashes.

It was England's first series victory since the infamous Bodyline Tour of 1932-33 and came after four drawn games - one of which was saved by a masterful rearguard fight by Trevor Bailey and Willie Watson.

The combined bowling skills of Fred Truman (pictured right) on the first day, and those of Jim Laker and Tony Lock in Australia's second innings, along with a strong last-day stand by Denis Compton and Bill Edrich, all helped steer England to an eight-wicket victory.

## AUGUST 13

# Quakes And Floods Hit Greece

More than 1,000 were killed and more than 100,000 made homeless in southern Greece today as the region was hit by a series of earthquakes and tidal waves caused by the tremors.

Worst affected were the Ionian Islands off the west coast, where a number of coastal villages on Corfu, Kefalinia and Zakinthos were all but destroyed.

# Nagy Releases UK 'Spy'

Confirmation of a thaw in Hungary's dealings with the West came today in the release of Edgar Sanders, the Briton gaoled for 13 years in 1949 as a spy.

The order to free Sanders could only have come directly from the new Prime Minister, Imre Nagy. It helps open the way to the increased dialogue and improved East-West relationships Nagy has said he wants to develop.

# Shah Flees Iran, Then Returns

**A MONTH OF YO-YO FORTUNES FOR THE SHAH OF IRAN:**

Ruler of his country in name only since the fiery nationalist Mohammed Mossadegh became Prime Minister in April 1951 and embarked on a series of increasingly bitter confrontations with Britain and other countries with interests in Iran's oil industry, the Shah and Queen Soraya were forced to flee to Rome on August 16 when an attempt to overthrow Mossadegh failed.

Within six days, however, the Shah was back in Tehran after a military coup led by General Fazollah Zahedi succeeded in ousting the premier, who was duly charged with treason for trying to usurp the Shah's authority.

A search of Iran's state treasury confirmed the worst. Mossadegh had run down the country's once-vast reserves. 'The situation is desperate', the Shah told world leaders as he appealed for aid. 'It's not a matter of months or even weeks, but of days.'

# Perry Proves Nice Guys Can Win

It's fair to say that Perry Como was one of the most important recording stars of the fifties. A breakdown of the biggest sellers in the US between 1954 and 1959 shows this relaxed, smooth-voiced former barber to have been outsold by only Elvis Presley and Pat Boone, with his 1954 hit *Wanted* racking up more sales in that period than *Rock Around The Clock* or Bobby Darin's mega-smash *Mack The Knife*.

This year saw the 40 year old poised to begin an international breakthrough after nine years as a major league player on home turf. Signed to RCA Victor in 1944, Como had notched up a remarkable 42 hits in the US without making a definite mark elsewhere. That all changed in 1953.

America's No 1 single in January and February, Como's *Don't Let The Stars Get In Your Eyes* crossed over to repeat the feat in Britain in February and kick-start a mutual love affair which would result in almost 50 more chart entries until well into the seventies.

As in the US, Como's multi-Emmy Award winning TV series acted as a sure-fire launch pad for many of those hits in Britain and, when rock 'n' roll arrived in 1955, he was smart enough to include the likes of Fats Domino, The Everly Brothers, Paul Anka and Fabian on his special-guest list and record a number of untypical uptempo singles to keep faith with younger

members of his fan club.

His effortless, laid-back style was not to everyone's taste, however. *Time* magazine memorably said he was so relaxed that 'he sometimes gives the impression of being made of sponge rubber with a core of Seconal'!

As he watched songs like *Catch A Falling Star, Magic Moments* and *Delaware* sell in their millions, Perry Como must have allowed himself a gentle smile and the slightest of shrugs.

## FREBERG PLAYS IT FOR LAUGHS

Comedy on record is awful hard to get right, if you think about it. It's reasonably easy to create something which tickles people's funnybones the first time they hear it, but it's nigh impossible to record humour folks will want to listen to repeatedly, or add to their record collection.

Stan Freberg was one of those rare comic talents who proved the exception to the rule, and the US No 1 he scored with *St George And The Dragonet* in October this year proved that in aces, being only the biggest of the 14 huge hits the 27 year old LA-born satirist enjoyed between 1951 and 1960.

A wonderful spoof on the smash TV series *Dragnet*, the single showcased Freberg's brilliance both as an impressionist and as a writer, skills he'd employed previously in 1951 with his spoof radio soap *John And Marsha* (banned as too suggestive in Britain) and his wonderfully cruel Johnnie Ray take-off *Try* in 1952.

Future international hits for the man who once supplied voices for Walt Disney, Paramount and Warner Bros cartoon characters and would become one of the most creative radio and TV ad directors in America, would include the timeless *Yellow Rose Of Texas,* (target: Mitch Miller singalongs), *Heartbreak Hotel* (rock 'n' roll in general, Elvis in particular), *The Banana Boat Song* (the calypso boom) and *The Old Payola Roll Blues* (rock 'n' roll again).

## JIMMY BOYD AND BEVERLEYS WITNESS YULE CANOODLE

The big Christmas hit of 1952-53 was one of those truly twee offerings which give treacle a bad name but somehow seem to survive their sheer awfulness to continue being recorded by future generations who ought to know better.

An American chart-topper in 1952 and Britain in 1953, the dubious credit for *I Saw Mommy Kissing Santa Claus* went to Jimmy Boyd who, thankfully, appears to have restricted his brief career to that and the equally-cloying *Tell Me A Story,* on which he chirruped winsomely to an ill-advised Frankie Laine. They don't, thank heavens, write songs like that anymore.

In Britain, the home-grown Beverley Sisters were close on little Jimmy's heels with their version of the yuletide snitching saga. Their first major chart entry, it would be followed by only a handful of hits in the next seven years, and two of them *(Little Drummer Boy* and *Little Donkey,* both in 1959) would be Christmas numbers.

Hugely popular with variety and radio audiences, these real-life sisters somehow never managed to translate their undoubted stage magic into vinyl anyone wanted to buy in quantity.

**Perry Como: poised for an international breakthrough**

# JFK Weds Society Beauty Jacqueline Bouvier

**FORGET THE CORONATION** of Queen Elizabeth - as far as the citizens of Newport, Rhode Island were concerned, the social event of 1953 was the wedding of the handsome young Senator John Fitzgerald Kennedy and high-society beauty Jacqueline Lee Bouvier.

Their marriage reception, which an estimated 3,000 people tried to gate-crash, had a Who's Who guest list befitting the eldest son of Joseph P. Kennedy, the prominent Boston millionaire financier and one-time US Ambassador to London.

Aged 36, the bridegroom is a Harvard graduate whose published thesis *Why England Slept* was a best-selling look at the pre-war rise of European fascism. A PT boat commander in the Pacific during WWII, Kennedy and his crew were rescued when his craft sank in 1943.

Entering politics in 1946, JFK won a seat in the House of Representatives, and in 1952 defeated the Republicans' elder statesman Henry Cabot Lodge to become Senator for Massachusetts.

His bride, who wore a classic ivory silk wedding gown, seemed taken aback by the huge crowd of onlookers. A noted beauty, she was, until recently a photographer for the *Washington Times-Herald*.

# Maclean Family Vanish

The mystery surrounding the disappearance of British diplomat Donald Maclean - who vanished in June 1951 with fellow Foreign Office expert Guy Burgess and is generally believed to be living secretly in Soviet Russia - deepened today. Swiss police have confirmed that Maclean's wife and three children have disappeared from the family home in Geneva. A complete search and border checks have not produced any results, but it is thought they have left Switzerland to join Maclean, wherever he is.

# Fox Unveil Widescreen 'Robe'

New York movie buffs got their first look at 20th Century Fox's much-publicized new Cinemascope format today with the first showing of *The Robe,* a solemn biblical epic which used the wide screen potential for dramatic impact to good effect. Although a starring vehicle for the well-established Victor Mature, the performance of his relatively-new co-star, the Welshman Richard Burton, is the one which stole the notices, the Oscar nomination and set Burton firmly on the road to superstardom.

**2:** In London's Olympia exhibition centre, the Radio Show included a new 27-inch TV, bigger by 15 inches than most current sets (see picture)

**3:** Florence Horsburgh became the Conservative Party's first-ever female cabinet minister when appointed Minister of Education

**6:** In Bonn, Konrad Adenauer re-elected Chancellor of West Germany

**10:** In Cyprus, 40 people killed in the island's worst-recorded earthquake

**12:** Nikita Khruschchev elected First Secretary of the USSR's Communist Party in Moscow

**24:** Rocky Marciano knocked out Roland LaStarza to retain his World heavyweight title

44

---

## SEPTEMBER 22

# Africans Reject Rhodesian Changes

**BLACK AFRICAN LEADERS** today rejected changes to the constitution of Northern Rhodesia fixed by a London conference which decided to continue white domination of the British colony's Legislative Council. Despite a lack of agreement on constitutional amendments, the British government has decided to impose them.

Although the number of African members of the Council has been increased from two to four, there will also be two more whites - a total of 14 - to ensure an overwhelming majority in all respects. African delegates, who had hoped for equal numbers of African and European members, say they cannot accept the changes. They represent 'a further extension of political power to the settlers' and will be resisted by all means.

---

## SEPTEMBER 20

# Sky News

Two air force pilots became headline news this month for very different reasons.
On September 20 a North Korean fighter pilot gave US intelligence services a great gift when he flew his MIG-15 Russian-built jet fighter over the border, landed near the South Korean capital Seoul and surrendered to Americans delighted to dismantle an enemy craft and question a man with military information.
The Libyan desert was the site chosen by Briton Michael Lithgow on September 25 when he took the controls of a Vickers Supermarine Swift F4 jet. The result - a new world record of 737.30 mph.

---

## SEPTEMBER 8

# USSR Recognizes Austria

The new regime in Moscow offered an olive branch of sorts to the West today when it announced its recognition of the Austrian Republic, so opening the way for a withdrawal of its troops from the country.

Like Germany, Austria has been divided into East-West administration zones since the end of WWII, with the capital Vienna dominated by roadblocks and check-points to mark the jealously-

defended enclaves.
Russia's recognition means the Soviets have abdicated all rights to base forces in Austria. A deal to arrange their departure and restore democracy is now negotiable.

*A new 27-inch television unveiled at The Radio Show, Olympia*

# Ike Bails Out Shah

President Eisenhower today authorized a $45 million (£14m) grant to the Shah of Iran in response to the emperor's plea for international aid last month.

Ike's generosity on behalf of the American people does not go unchallenged. There are mutterings from some who recall the Shah's extravagant wedding in 1951, the most memorable highlight of which was Queen Soraya's dress, encrusted with $1.5 million worth of diamonds.

OCT

# Ford's Popular Wins New UK Price War

**FORD'S BRITISH DIVISION -** runaway winners of the 1952 battle for supremacy in the low-price car market - sprang a surprise on main rivals Austin and Standard today with the launch of the aptly-named Popular (pictured left).

A re-working of the original Ford Anglia, the Popular is the world's cheapest four-cylinder family saloon at only £390 ($1100) including tax. This easily beats Austin's two-door A30, which costs £475, and the four-door Standard Eight, which is priced at £481.

The Popular's launch comes only a month after Ford unveiled its new 11 hp Anglia - a £511 purchase wrongly said to signal the company's move away from austerity motoring - and an updated Prefect.

Britain has witnessed a massive increase in motor sales since petrol rationing ended in May 1950. The Popular helps make a car an attainable dream for many more British families.

# World Mourns Ferrier And Bax

The arts world was saddened today by the death at the age of only 41 of the British-born operatic contralto Kathleen Ferrier. She had developed inoperable cancer. Ferrier, who began her adult life as a switchboard operator and did not perform in opera until 1946, was a unique performer whose popularity was not confined to opera-lovers. Her versions of classic ballads were best-sellers worldwide and her solo concert recitals helped introduce many to the world of great music.

The news was the second blow for British music-lovers this month. On October 3, Sir Arnold Bax, the 70 year old composer who was Master of The Queen's Music, died after a long illness. His successor to the royal-appointed post is to be Sir Arthur Bliss.

# Shah Clamps Communists

The Shah of Iran's new government indicated its long-term intentions towards dissidents of any persuasion when it began a purge of the Tudeh, Iran's communist party, in the capital Tehran today. Hundreds of known members and suspected sympathizers were rounded up in raids, the ferocity of which appalled even the most hardened veteran Iran-watchers.

# British Guiana Turmoil

Threat of an imminent Communist coup forced the British government to move troops and warships to its South American colony of British Guiana this month.

The force began moving from West Indian bases on October 6, three days before local government administrators suspended the constitution and declared a state of martial law.

While troops moved into strategic positions around the colony, police began to hunt down those believed to be involved in the coup conspiracy. On October 27, the British arrested and interned five key members of the left-wing People's Progressive Party.

## ARRIVALS
**Born this month:**

**12:** David Threlfall, British actor
**12:** Tom Petty, US rock singer/songwriter/guitarist
**14:** Roland Butcher, West Indies cricketer
**28:** Mark James, British golfer, Ryder Cup player

## DEPARTURES
**Died this month:**
**3:** Sir Arnold Edward Trevor Bax, composer, Master of The Queen's Music *(see main story)*
**8:** Kathleen Mary Ferrier, opera singer *(see main story)*

## OCTOBER 8

# Yugoslav Fury As Italy Takes Trieste

**YUGOSLAVIA'S PRESIDENT TITO** voiced his fury at today's announcement that the United States and Britain are to withdraw their troops from the Italian-Yugoslav border region around Trieste, handing control of the zone they've governed since the end of WWII to Italy.

Both Yugoslavia - who occupy the other Free Territory of Trieste zone with 10,000 troops - and Italy lay claim to the whole territory, a claim which the Italian government now intends to pursue with a local referendum.

Until now Italy has merely policed the British-US Zone with a British-trained force. President Tito condemned the UK-US decision, saying he would appeal to the UN. Windows in British, American and Italian buildings were smashed by crowds in the Yugoslav capital Belgrade.

Under the terms of an original peace treaty, Trieste was supposed to become a UN-administered independent nation, but the Communists and the West have never been able to hammer out terms for the new state.

## OCTOBER 14

# Israel Attacks Jordan

International reaction against today's Israeli army attack on three Jordanian villages the Tel Aviv government say are centres for Palestinian guerrillas, is to strain even the special relationship between Israel and the United States.

First to condemn the raids, in which 56 villagers and alleged terrorists were killed, were Britain and France. Both called in their Israeli ambassadors to stress their outrage.

Only a month later, on November 16, the United States would join France and Britain in a UN resolution vote condemning the raid to complete Israel's isolation in world opinion.

# Doctors Slam Stilettos

The hit of this year's fashion scene and a vital element in the wardrobe of any woman with pretensions to style, the stiletto heel has come in for fierce criticism from doctors on both sides of the Atlantic having to deal with a rise in ankle and foot injuries.

No-one disputes that the long thin heels (hence their name), some of which can be as much as five inches high, can be very elegant. But they are, doctors agree, completely unnatural, causing women to carry off a precarious and often-unsuccessful balancing act while their toes are crammed painfully into the shoe.

OCT

# JANUARY 1,
# HANK WILLIAMS: TRAGIC KING OF COUNTRY

Hank Williams was the first real country superstar, his legend in life made larger by frequent bouts of illness and clashes with the establishment when his drinking became uncontrolled, his immortality guaranteed by the continued popularity of the songs he wrote, many of which remain much-covered staples all round the world.

Born Hiram King Williams (in September 1923) and raised near Montgomery, Alabama, Hank signed to the newly-formed MGM label in 1947 and, with his band The Drifting Cowboys, joined the cast of the influential Louisiana Hayride radio show, even though his drink problem was already evident. In 1949, after scoring a big hit with *Lovesick Blues,* he was invited to join The Grand Ole Opry.

Williams had, in fact, had an earlier hit with *Move It On Over,* but it was *Lovesick Blues* which started an almost unbroken run of Top 10 singles which was to continue long after his death. Williams smashed every existing industry statistic in that first year, racking up Top 10 entries with *Wedding Belles, Mind Your Own Business, You're Gonna Change* and *My Bucket's Got A Hole In It.*

There's little doubt that constant pain from a back injury he'd suffered when he was thrown from a horse at the age of 17 was the cause of Williams' drinking, but the Opry organizers were less interested in causes than effect, and they fired him from the show in 1952, even though further hits like *Cold Cold Heart* (also a pop hit for Tony Bennett), *Hey Good Lookin', Crazy Love, Honky Tonk Blues, Half As Much, Jambalaya*

**Hank Williams: the first country superstar**

(covered by Jo Stafford) and *Settin' The Woods On Fire* in 1951 and 1952 made him the hottest property in town.

Throwing himself into self-promotion, Williams divorced his wife Audrey Sheppard, married Billie Jean Jones and re-staged his wedding on a number of occasions to huge crowds who paid for the privilege.

While the last year of his life proved incredibly lucrative, Williams was paying a terrible price for continued success. Pain and drink combined to shrink his always-slender frame into a gaunt skeleton, and while many were shocked and saddened, few were surprised when news came that he'd died in the back of his chauffeur-driven car on January 1, *en route* to a show in Canton, Ohio.

More than 20,000 people attended his funeral in Montgomery. With the irony for which the music world is renowned, the single in the charts when he died was *I'll Never Get Out Of This World Alive*. Within months it would be followed by *Your Cheatin' Heart, Take These Chains From My Heart, I Won't Be Home No More* and *Weary Blues From Waitin'*. Elected to the Country Music Hall of Fame in 1961, Hank Williams helped transform hillbilly music into showbiz.

## MAY 16
# DJANGO REINHARDT

The first non-American to become a major jazz star and influence a generation of guitarists with his fusion of jazz and gipsy *tzigane* traditions, Django Reinhardt was born in a caravan in Belgium. Initially a violinist, he switched to guitar after a fire mutilated his left hand, leaving him with only two functioning fingers with which to develop a unique technique.

In 1934 he and violinist Stephane Grappeli founded the seminal all-string Quintet of The Hot Club de France. When it disbanded in 1939, the group had created a legacy of fine recordings marked especially by Reinhardt's glittering and intricate playing.

A regular guest on European recordings by US stars between 1935-39, Reinhardt became a popular visitor to America after the war, most notably appearing in concert with Duke Ellington at Carnegie Hall in 1946. His death at the age of 43 was sudden, unexpected and tragically premature for a man who, despite being unable to read music, had created so much that was brilliant.

## MARCH 23
# RAOUL DUFY

One of France's most distinctive modern painters, Raoul Dufy was born in Le Havre in 1877 and moved to Paris in 1900 to concentrate on developing his skills and commercial outlets for his paintings.

Initially attracted and influenced by the brilliant colours used by the *Fauvists*, he later came under Cézanne's sway to arrive at his own decorative style by the late 1920s.

A lively draughtsman, Dufy combined a clever use of colour with fine drawings to create charming watercolours and oils of fashionable resorts, race meetings and flowers.

## JULY 6
# NANCI GRIFFITH

A leading light in the so-called New Country boom of the early 1980s, Nanci Griffith was born in Seguin, Texas and was raised on a strong diet of folk music.

After a spell as a kindergarten teacher following graduation from the University of Texas, Griffith turned professional in 1977, releasing her first album a year later. A shrewd and self-managed artist, Griffith established a highly-successful publishing company to maximise earnings from the many songs she's written and which have become huge hits for the likes of the more-commercial Suzy Bogguss and Kathy Mattea.

Prepared to take huge risks, Griffith's recording career has seen her working with other acts as musically diverse as Irish folk band The Chieftains and English rock star Rod Argent. More an album artist than singles star, she is a genuine superstar in Britain and Europe, where she regularly sells out the biggest concert venues.

NOV

# Smog-Bound London Masks Up

**IT'S ALL VERY WELL FOR** novelists and popular songwriters to wax lyrical about foggy London town, but today's decision to make smog masks available via the National Health Service is proof that air pollution in the British capital, and some industrial cities, is nothing to sing about.

Smog - an often-deadly mixture of smoke and fog created by the widespread use of 'dirty' coal in domestic fires and unfiltered industrial chimney discharges being held at ground level by the pressure-cooker effect of winter fog - is recognized as a special danger to asthmatics and others already suffering heart or lung diseases.

From today, doctors can prescribe either of two masks. Both have refill pads of cotton tissue and gauze, though the British Medical Association considers neither any more than a stop-gap measure.

Moves are being made to clean up British air and eliminate smog, and calls are increasing for the government to legislate for the enforced use of smokeless fuels in domestic fires.

# TV With Ads For UK

Britain is to be allowed commercial television, with the BBC losing its TV monopoly as a new independent corporation grants licences to production companies drawing their revenue from advertisements.

Announcing the move today in a White Paper bill, the Conservative government say that the new TV stations will be confined to no more than six minutes of ads in each hour of broadcasting.

To help the BBC compete with the newcomers, the annual TV licence fee is to be increased from £2 ($6) to £3. Despite opposition from the socialist Labour Party, the government's plans were approved by the House of Lords on November 26.

# Hungary Thrash England

A dark day for English soccer: the national team, never beaten at Wembley Stadium by a foreign team, were humiliated by a dazzling Hungarian side who thrashed them 6-3. With commentators grasping wildly to describe the outstanding skills of Hungary's centre-forward Hidekguti (who scored three) and captain Ferenc Puskas (who slotted in two), it was obvious that the visitors' superiority could have resulted in an even bigger defeat. A gloomy post mortem is about to begin.

# Polio Virus Snapped

The fight against polio led by American specialist Dr. Jonas Salk has long been hampered by researchers not actually having seen the virus to establish its construction, and so do more than develop a vaccine to combat its effects.

That breakthrough came today when the virus was identified and photographed for the first time. It gives the Salk team a huge advantage in their quest for a solution to the water-borne killer.

## ARRIVALS

**Born this month:**

**3:** Roseanne, US comedy actress, writer, TV producer *(Roseanne)*

**7:** Lucinda Green (née Prior-Palmer), British Olympic horsewoman

**16:** Griff Rhys Jones, UK comic TV and stage actor

**21:** Tina Brown, UK born editor of *New Yorker* magazine

## DEPARTURES

**Died this month:**

**8:** Ivan Alexeyevich Bunin, Russian poet

**9:** King Abdul Aziz Ibn Saud, founder and ruler of the modern state of Saudi Arabia; Dylan Thomas, Welsh poet *(see main story)*

**27:** Eugene Gladstone O'Neill, US playwright *(A Long Day's Journey Into Night, etc)*

**30:** Francis Picabia, French artist

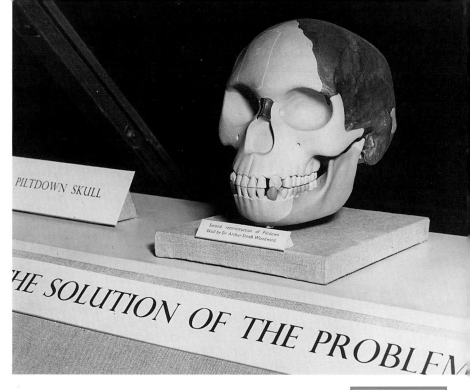

PILTDOWN SKULL

Second reconstruction of Piltdown Skull by Sir Arthur Smith Woodward.

THE SOLUTION OF THE PROBLEM

# Piltdown Man Was Hoax

NOVEMBER 21

A skull 'found' in a quarry near the southern English village of Piltdown, Sussex almost 40 years ago, and long hailed as that of a possible missing link between Man and his ape ancestors, was a put-together fake, it was revealed today.

New tests by London scientists using procedures not available when the skull was first presented to the Natural History Museum and put on display in 1913, have proved 'Piltdown Man' was in fact a union of parts of different animals from separate historical periods.

# Poet Dylan Does Not Go Gently

**DYLAN THOMAS,** the Welsh-born poet notorious for his heavy drinking, wild lifestyle and rejection of authority, went out in typical style today - he collapsed and died at New York's Chelsea Hotel after a lengthy drinking bout. He was only 39 years old.

In America for a lecture tour, Thomas had enthralled as many young fans as he had outraged those in the arts establishment. Even they had to admit that the hell-raiser was a remarkable poet when a volume of his collected works became an international best-seller last year.

A regular broadcaster from the BBC's London headquarters, Thomas revolutionized the medium with his dramatic magnum opus *Under Milk Wood,* a creation he called 'a play for voices'. Never intended to be performed as an actors-with-scenery production, Thomas had supervized and appeared in a staged reading with American actors at the Kaufmann Auditorium of the Young Men's Hebrew Association in New York in May 1953, but it would not be broadcast by the BBC, with a Welsh cast led by Richard Burton, until January 1954.

It is rare for a living poet's words to pass into everyday use, but Thomas achieved that with lines from a poem-epitaph for his father - 'Do not go gentle into that good night...Rage, rage against the dying of the light'.

## French Take Dien Bien Phu

The strategic South Vietnamese Dien Bien Phu plateau was captured from the North Vietnamese Viet Minh today by a French force made up of crack paratroops and Foreign Legionnaires.

The mass airdrop from Dakota transporters and armoured helicopters took the Communist forces of North Vietnam leader Ho Chi Minh by surprise. While the French lost 14 men in what was code-named 'Operation Castor', more than 60 Viet Minh were killed.

Dien Bien Phu will give French commander General Navarre a prime offensive base once his engineers repair a nearby Japanese-built airfield and he has replaced his victorious shock troops with infantry and artillery.

## McCarthy Accuses Truman

Eyebrows shot up in Washington today at the latest outrageous claim by the increasingly controversial Senator Joe McCarthy, chairman of the Senate House Committee investigating alleged infiltration of American society by communists and communism.

For the past three years the Wisconsin politician has masterminded and overseen what many consider to be a vicious witch-hunt. The enforced exile of Charlie Chaplin in April is a prime example of McCarthy's power and his selection of high-profile victims to help guarantee maximum press and TV coverage.

NOV

# Nobel Prize For Winston Churchill

**IT IS NOT UNUSUAL** for politicians to be awarded a Nobel Prize, the world's most prestigious award for distinction in a number of fields.

Usually it's the much-coveted Peace Prize which comes their way. The award of the 1953 Nobel Prize for Literature to British Prime Minister Sir Winston Churchill to recognize his exhaustive multi-volume *History of The English Speaking Peoples* is confirmation of the intellectual brilliance of a man whose teachers dismissed as a lazy dullard.

Described in the official citation as 'a Caesar who wields the stylus of a Cicero', Sir Winston was represented at the Stockholm ceremony by his wife. He was in Bermuda for a conference.

A prolific author throughout his life, despite the many years he'd devoted to public service as a constituency Member of Parliament, minister of state or international statesman, Churchill's history of World War II would take up six volumes, while his biography of his ancestor the Duke of Marlborough took four.

While the Literature Prize is normally given to a poet or novelist, Sir Winston confessed he'd only ever written one novel - something he admitted 'I have consistently urged my friends to abstain from reading'!

# Britain Gets Building

Although it's been eight years since the end of World War II, the re-building of Britain is only now beginning to transform the country the way its leaders envisaged - and promised - in the first heady days of peacetime.

With many of Britain's industrial centres decimated by air-raids and reconstruction of its manufacturing heartland an initial priority, the overwhelming need for new and replacement housing is finally being tackled.

Today's government figures - a record 301,000 new homes have been built in the past year, according to Housing Minister Harold Macmillan - are confirmation that the problem is being tackled.

Government spending on housing is now only exceeded by the defence budget, and a relaxation of rent controls has been introduced to help defray the costs incurred by landlords repairing or improving properties.

## DECEMBER 7

# Supreme Court Considers Race Laws

A momentous day in American history as members of the US Supreme Court began to consider state laws which enforce racial segregation in schools.

An intrinsic element in the everyday life of southern states, where the separation of white and black communities is universal, segregation of schools is a nationwide phenomenon which many believe is unacceptable in the second half of the 20th century.

Chief Justice Earl Warren is the man who will have the unenviable task, in May 1954, of overturning the 1896 ruling that education could be 'separate but equal' and begin a lengthy and often-violent confrontation between southern whites and federal authorities attempting to enforce the Supreme Court's ruling.

**2:** Two million British engineering workers staged a 24 hour strike for higher pay

**4:** Geologists discovered a large oilfield in North-Western Australia

**9:** Kenya is to receive a £10 million ($30m) aid grant from Britain, it was announced

**10:** In Oslo, Finland, 1953 Nobel Peace Prize awarded to George Marshall, American creator of the post-war Marshall Plan to aid the reconstruction of Europe

**19:** In Tehran, The Shah of Iran called a general election

## ARRIVALS

**Born this month:**

**8:** Kim Basinger, US film actress (Batman, Nine and ½ Weeks, etc)

**16:** Stephanie Lawrence, British pop singer

**20:** Mark Kaplan, classical violinist

## DEPARTURES

**Died this month:**

**19:** Robert Millikan, US physicist

**DECEMBER 25**

# Soviets Execute Police Chief Beria

Stalin's secret police chief Lavrenti Beria followed countless thousands of his purge victims today in Moscow when he and six other senior officers were shot by a firing squad after a secret trial found him guilty of plotting to seize power and being a Western agent.

Arrested in June and undoubtedly treated with the same ruthlessness he'd consistently displayed through the years he disposed of all perceived enemies of his boss, Beria was said to have admitted to plotting the overthrow of Prime Minister Malenkov in the weeks following Stalin's death. No-one took the 'western agent' accusations seriously.

**DECEMBER 29**

# Viet Minh Reach Mekong

The Viet Minh forces of North Vietnam confirmed the worst fears of Western analysts today when they reached South Vietnam's main artery, the Mekong River, from bases in neighboring Thailand.

It is precisely the scenario predicted in May when French intelligence confirmed that the Viet Minh had established arms and supply centres along the Thai border. The Mekong River is arguably the single most important 'highway' in a country with limited roads, and reaches the sea near the South Vietnam capital, Saigon.

# Insulin Breakthrough Puts UK At The Forefront Of World Science

**HOT ON THE HEELS** of the Watson-Crick team's construction of DNA in April, another Cambridge-based scientist - the biochemist Dr. Frederick Sanger - has produced another breakthrough with immense implications for world medicine in general, and diabetics in particular.

Sanger's achievement, after eight years of research, is the first-ever full chemical analysis of a protein, in this case insulin, the hormone which controls the level of sugar in blood and which diabetics lack.

The problem facing Sanger and other biochemists is that proteins consist of different combinations of around 20 sub-units, called amino acids. Joined together in long chains, their structure is the key to a protein's function.

Sanger established insulin's structure by breaking it down into smaller and smaller fragments until he could determine the order in which they fitted together. His research was not helped by the fact that insulin, with only 50 amino acids, is a relatively simple protein.

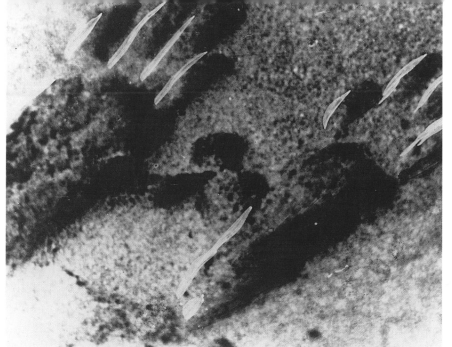

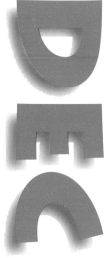

# Yeti Hunt Begins

DECEMBER 31

A British-funded expedition arrived in New Delhi today, en route for Nepal where it will carry out the first official organized hunt for the mysterious Himalayan creature known to locals as the Yeti, but popularly known in the West as The Abominable Snowman.

Reported sightings of the Yeti, said to be a large, hairy, ape-like animal which lives high in the mountains between Nepal and Tibet, include testimony from Everest mountaineers whose sobriety and common-sense are accepted.

The publication of a photograph said to show a Yeti footprint in the snow (pictured above), caused enough controversy this year for the expedition to be formed.

## YOUR 1953 HOROSCOPE

Unlike most Western horoscope systems which group astrological signs into month-long periods based on the influence of 12 constellations, the Chinese believe that those born in the same year of their calendar share common qualities, traits and weaknesses with one of 12 animals - Rat, Ox, Tiger, Rabbit, Dragon, Snake, Horse, Sheep, Monkey, Rooster, Dog or Pig.

They also allocate the general attributes of five natural elements - Earth, Fire, Metal, Water, Wood - and an overall positive or negative aspect to each sign to summarize its qualities.

If you were born between January 27, 1952 and February 13, 1953, you are a Dragon. As this book is devoted to the events of 1953, let's take a look at the sign which governs those born between February 14 that year and February 2, 1954 - The Year of The Snake

# THE SNAKE
## (FEBRUARY 14, 1953 - FEBRUARY 2, 1954)
### ELEMENT: WATER  ASPECT: ▬

The Snake represents the sign of wisdom, and those born under its influence are cautious, mysterious and can easily be ignored. However, Snakes have a strong, charismatic presence, a bewitching charm and are said to be endowed with wisdom and deep philosophical understanding.

Snakes are driven by a strong sense of destiny and a life mission. They are serious types - deep thinkers who could never be considered shallow or frivolous, taking time to formulate their ideas and opinions. While they command respect, people don't always feel at ease around Snakes, who can be treacherous creatures who never forgive or forget.

There's a certain duality in Snakes' personalities which makes them hard to figure out. As much as Snakes can be strong and ready for action, at some point they can also be very cautious and calculating. Snakes are seen as mysterious and enigmatic because of their ability to put their fingers right on the button. With their great intuition, Snakes possess all the ingredients to make a mystic.

The Snake's love of the arts - especially music - comes from this inner sensitivity. Artistic or not, Snakes tend to flourish in the world of art and are attracted to any expression of creativity and the inner self. Being careful about material things, Snakes are not considered extravagant.

Snakes project the best self-image that they can, and though sometimes described as vain, they have a quite magical ability to make the very best out of the most mediocre and are notoriously good-looking with elegant and stylish clothes.

Attracted by success and power, Snakes are extremely selective in their choice of close companions. Although deeply passionate and demanding, they could not possibly be described as butch or aggressive. Very sensual, Snakes turn their tension inwards.

More concerned with the analysis of character and the deeper levels of understanding the human condition, Snakes can also be treacherous and will do anything to save their own skin.

## FAMOUS SNAKES

**Stefan Edberg,**
tennis champion

**Ernest Borgnine,**
Oscar-winning film actor

**Tom Conti,**
film actor

**Jacqueline Kennedy Onassis**

**André Previn,**
conductor, musician

**Victoria Wood,**
comedienne, actress, writer

**David Hasselhoff,**
actor (*Baywatch*), rock singer, director